A Guide To Family Intervention

Mary Bratton

Health Communications, Inc.
Pompano Beach, Florida

Mary Bratton
Family Therapist
Perrysburg, Ohio

Library of Congress Cataloging-in-Publication Data
   Filed

© 1987   Mary Bratton

ISBN 0-932194-52-4

Health Communications, Inc.
1721 Blount Road
Pompano Beach, Florida 33069

Cover design by Reta Kaufman

To Drew
who risked and cared and supported

With Thanks To
Lorraine Mason and Sue Wisniewski
for their help and encouragement

Intervention is more than an event, a single confrontation with the chemically dependent person. Intervention is a process that begins a lifelong journey to recovery for both the chemically dependent person and the people who care about him/her. This book will guide you step by step as you travel the road to intervention, offering hope and encouragement and support as signposts along the way.

Contents

Part I

To The Family

Part II

To The Therapist 53

Part I

To The Family

1

The First Step

Alcohol and/or drugs are causing problems for someone you care about. Sometimes you feel angry and are sure that you cannot go on much longer. Sometimes you feel guilty and are sure that you are over-reacting. Sometimes you feel ashamed even to think about what has been happening, much less talk about it to someone else. You want to help but you feel helpless.

Your very concern about the drinking and/or drug use is one of the best indicators that there really is a problem. And somehow you know that the problem will simply not go away by itself.

Perhaps you have begun to learn that there are things caring people can do to help. Perhaps you have already found a counselor and begun to plan an intervention. Perhaps you have never even heard that word before. But you know you just cannot let the person you care about go on destroying him or herself.

This book will call on you to show a special kind of love and a special brand of courage. It will call on you to commit your time, your energy and your emotions to learning, training and changing. There may be times when it seems easier to forget and run away. There may be times when it seems easier to continue to endure. You may feel frightened and confused. Answers and encouragement lie ahead.

You have just begun your own journey out of helplessness and hopelessness. At the end of the road to intervention wait freedom and recovery, for you and for the person you love.

Intervention . . . One Family's Story

Meg hung up the phone, shaking. After months of debating with herself about her husband's drinking, she had finally taken action, and she was scared. The last few years seemed a series of lonely nights, wondering when or if Jeff would come home from the club, nasty and blaming and ready to argue, or apologetic and ashamed and needing to be helped to bed. But she knew there had been good times, too, picnics and barbeques and vacations when the family seemed happy and carefree and almost normal again. Those were the times when Meg was convinced Jeff couldn't really be an alcoholic. Their home in the suburbs, their two wonderful children, Jeff's job as a top insurance salesman, his dedication to coaching their son's soccer team, their friends, their whole life screamed denial at that awful word — alcoholic.

Yet she knew that the bad times had begun to outnumber the good. She knew that poised and pretty 16-year-old Jenny was spending more and more time in her room, that happy-go-lucky 14-year-old Josh was turning angry and sullen, that Jeff was going into work late sometimes and beginning to miss evening appointments with clients. The celebration after the last soccer victory had been a nightmare. Even her own work as a nurse was suffering. Last week she had been so exhausted and distracted after another night of waiting up for Jeff that she failed to record a doctor's order in a patient chart — a mistake that mortified her and earned her a stiff reprimand from her supervisor.

Meg had to admit that she was losing her husband to alcohol. She felt helpless and angry and confused. She wondered if she was doing something wrong, or if there was something wrong with her, because her husband needed to drink so much. Alone, she hadn't been able to fight the hold alcohol seemed to be gaining on Jeff. Time and time again she felt Jeff had the drinking licked, only to see each step forward followed by two steps backward.

Finally she had done what the counselor advised. She had reached out from her silence and isolation and shame to seek help for Jeff — help he didn't even know was about to be offered. She had asked their children, and Jeff's boss Malcolm, and his sister Lisa, and Tom, Jeff's best friend since college days and now his assistant soccer coach, to be part of an intervention team. Her whispered call to the counselor put the last piece of the puzzle into place. Jeff had just agreed to go with her the next morning to talk to the counselor about his "drinking problem". He hadn't agreed happily or willingly because he didn't agree that his drinking was anything more than "what everybody else does". But after the last episode at the soccer banquet, he really didn't dare refuse just one session with a counselor.

However, Jeff didn't know what awaited him in the counselor's office. He didn't know about all the other people who would be there prepared to confront him with evidence of his problems with alcohol and determined to insist that he get treatment. If all went well, Jeff would be a patient in the treatment center tomorrow, but tonight Meg was frightened and anxious, afraid for herself, afraid for the other people involved and, most of all, afraid for Jeff.

The team had trained with the counselor for almost a month now without Jeff's knowledge. Meg had told Jeff she was seeing a counselor to help her deal with his drinking, but she hadn't mentioned the others who had been coming, too. In fact, she had been surprised that everyone had agreed to help. But as they talked together in the counselor's office, they all expressed surprise and then alarm as they shared and recognized the many problems alcohol was causing for Jeff and the many secrets they had all been keeping from one another. They learned that alcoholism is a disease, and they realized they had all been blaming themselves and protecting Jeff while the illness slowly destroyed him.

Meg held on to her newfound knowledge of everyone's love and concern for Jeff. Even Jeff's boss, strong and austere Malcolm, had choked up yesterday when they rehearsed what they would say to Jeff during intervention. Meg hoped she wouldn't have to tell Jeff that she planned to leave him if he refused to get help, but she knew she was prepared to do that out of love for him, to help him choose to get well, and she knew everyone else on the team supported her decision. She hoped Malcolm wouldn't have to threaten to fire Jeff, but she knew Malcolm was prepared to do that if it became necessary, and she supported his decision. And most of all, she hoped that the last member of the team, a man the counselor introduced to them only as Charlie, a recovering alcoholic, could get through to Jeff even if the rest of the team couldn't.

The drive to the counselor's office seemed endless. Meg saw Jeff's hesitation as he walked into the room and looked at all the important people in his life waiting to talk to him. She expected him to turn around and run, but when he crossed the room and sat down, she finally began to believe what the counselor had been telling them about the overwhelming power of an intervention team.

Jeff agreed with the counselor's request that he listen without responding to what everyone had to say.

Malcolm, Jeff's boss, started speaking. Malcolm talked about what a wonderful salesman Jeff was and how proud he was to have Jeff associated with the firm. But Jeff couldn't argue when Malcolm began to present the facts about Jeff's drinking:

"Last Monday you called to say you'd be in late to work — you had the flu. I cancelled your 10:00 o'clock appointment for you — an appointment with the Ferguson account that was important to the agency and really a fantastic break for you. I cancelled the appointment because I believed you were sick. But when you came in at noon, your eyes were puffy and bloodshot and you smelled of alcohol — even the receptionist mentioned it to me. You sat at your desk with your head in your hands, made a few phone calls, and left the office early.

"Jeff, the commission on that account alone would pay your salary for three or four months. Ferguson was upset and inconvenienced, and he still hasn't rescheduled the appointment. I was disappointed and frustrated about the account, and I felt guilty about covering up for you with Ferguson. More than that, I was embarrassed to have your co-workers see you like that. I hate to see what alcohol is doing to the fine agent I hired eight years ago.

"Jeff, alcohol is beginning to cause serious problems for you on your job, and I'm here today to ask you to get help."

Slowly they went around the circle, each sharing the ways they saw alcohol affecting and changing the competent and caring Jeff they remembered. Jeff's sister talked about missing her brother at family gatherings. Jeff's friend, Tom, told Jeff how embarrassed he was when he needed to hide Jeff's drinking from the other soccer parents. Josh told his dad he felt ashamed when Jeff slurred his words while giving out awards at the soccer banquet.

When Meg's turn came, she talked about her worry and fear during the long evening hours Jeff spent at the club. She recounted the times he had promised to quit drinking and then been unable to keep his promise.

It wasn't until Jenny spoke that Meg realized the depth of damage Jeff's drinking had done to their family. Even when they rehearsed, Jenny hadn't fully shared her pain. But with the rest of the team risking together she was able to say to Jeff, "Dad, I love you, but when you drink I'm scared to leave you alone for fear something terrible might happen to you. Last month I cancelled a date for a party at the last minute because Mom and Josh were out shopping and you were home drinking. Instead, I sat upstairs on my bed listening to you stumble around downstairs. I heard the refrigerator door open every time you got another beer. I wanted to come down and talk to you, but I knew I couldn't talk to the alcohol. I felt scared and lonely, but at least I knew I was there to take care of you if you needed me. But I don't want it to be like that. I want us to be family again. I want my dad back. Please, please get help."

Jeff had trouble looking at any of the people in the room while they were speaking, but Meg knew he was listening and she could see his denial slowly crumbling.

At the end Jeff looked up only at Charlie when he said, "I'm a recovering alcoholic . . ." And it was to Charlie that Jeff gave his agreement to enter treatment immediately.

At that moment Meg knew she had done all that she could do. She and the rest of the intervention team had given Jeff a chance at recovery — recovery itself was now up to Jeff.

2

Why An Intervention?

Alcoholism or chemical dependency is a disease, a primary, progressive, chronic, fatal disease. It is a *primary* disease, a disease in its own right, a describable and identifiable condition that causes other physical problems, like liver damage or malnutrition. It gets worse over time, which makes it *progressive*. It is *chronic*; it remains in the body, whether or not it is activated by the triggering substance — alcohol or another drug. It can be arrested, but it cannot be cured. And it is *fatal*. Untreated, chemical dependency kills.

Those four words — primary, progressive, chronic and fatal — can be used to describe many illnesses — some types of heart disease, cancer and diabetes. In fact, diabetes and chemical dependency are much alike. Everybody eats sugar; some people have trouble with sugar because their bodies are different. Likewise, most people drink alcohol or take some other mood-altering chemical at some time in their lives. About one out of ten people who use those chemicals have trouble with them because their bodies are different. Although that is a very simple explanation, there is much medical evidence and research to support it.

The Number One Drug

When alcohol is the substance involved, this condition is called alcoholism. And alcohol is still the most common mood-altering substance available to people. In fact, it was about the only available one for centuries. However, as more and more tranquilizers and pain medications have been invented and become widely used, these drugs, too, have begun to cause problems for certain people. Alcohol is also a chemical, and a more accurate description of the disease is probably chemical dependency. What has happened is very much like what would have occurred had apple pie been the only sugar source available for centuries. It would have triggered diabetes in certain people. But then if vanilla ice cream and chocolate cake had been discovered, they, too, would have begun to cause the same problems for certain people that apple pie had been causing all along.

If the two diseases are so similar, then why does the diabetic have relatively less trouble recognizing his problem and getting help, while the chemically dependent person seems to fight to stay sick against insuperable odds? The difference lies in the nature of the substances themselves.

Sugar does little more than alter the body. But when that happens the diabetic can often identify the symptoms and seek treatment. Alcohol and other mood-altering drugs affect not only the body; they change the brain. They change the way people think, the way they feel, the way they perceive reality. Even a social drinker knows the girls get prettier and the music gets better as the party progresses!

In the social user these emotional and perceptual changes are mild and enjoyable; for the dependent user they become immense and cataclysmic as the disease progresses.

The chemically dependent person is affected by his drug in three major ways. First, the drug itself creates a tight denial system that convinces the user that nothing is wrong. The drug is seen not as the problem but rather as the solution to other problems. A wealth of excuses and a wall of blame are erected to defend the using and explain it away. Second, the drug alters reality. At the times the chemically dependent person is most impaired, he pictures himself walking and talking normally and in total control. Finally, the chemically dependent person often experiences blackouts, those periods when under the influence of the drug, he functions but later does not remember what he did or said. The drug is causing him to deny part of reality, to see another part of reality in a very distorted way, and to forget the rest. How can he see he has a problem?

The Myth of Hitting Bottom

We used to believe that the chemically dependent person had to be allowed to progress along the destructive path of the disease until some crisis occurred spontaneously to motivate recovery. You have probably heard that old saying, "An alcoholic has to 'hit bottom' before he can be helped." Unfortunately, some chemically dependent people hit bottom as they hit a school bus loaded full of children, or as they hit a bridge abutment. They die, and they die unnecessarily.

We have learned that we don't have to wait that long; we don't have to wait for the natural crisis that may never occur. Instead, caring people can create a crisis, an "artificial bottom", sufficient to force the chemically dependent person to seek help. This is called *intervention*.

3

What Is Intervention?

Intervention is a planned, orchestrated confrontation with the chemically dependent person, done by the significant people in his life, people armed with factual, non-judgmental data about the drinking and/or using, specific treatment options and consequences, and their own care and concern. This managed crisis is often enough to break through the defenses created by the illness and initiate recovery.

"But," you may be saying to yourself, "he has already been confronted; we have all tried until we are exhausted."

Intervention is predicated on the understanding that the chemically dependent person may have been approached many times before, by family, friends and even employers. However, these confrontations have typically been attempted by one person angry or upset enough to bring up one or two incidents and then demand that the chemically dependent person "cut down" or "use will power".

One person will be brushed off: "You're just imagining things." One or two incidents will be dismissed: "That doesn't happen every time I use." And the chemically dependent person is prepared for anger. In fact, he may turn it back on you and you may end up defending yourself, rather than talking about the drinking and/or using. Finally the plea to cut down or stop spontaneously is fruitless in the face of a primary, progressive, chronic, fatal disease. It may be as well to feed a diabetic a piece of pie and ask her to control her blood sugar with will power.

Combined Power

Instead, an intervention will mobilize the combined power of everyone in the chemically dependent person's life. It will paint a picture for him, with fact after fact of the effects alcohol and drugs are having on his life. It will be based in love, concern and a genuine understanding of the disease, rather than in anger and a need for revenge. And, most important, it will offer concrete help and a real hope for recovery.

Intervention will allow you to smash through the wall of defenses the disease has created around the chemically dependent person and then stand ready, with arms outstretched in love, to catch him as he falls.

4

Where Should We Go For Intervention?

Although some families have accomplished intervention on their own, it seems much easier to work with a counselor who is trained in the intervention process. If you are already working with a counselor in a professional setting, so much the better. If not, now is the time to begin seeking one out. The Yellow Pages of your phone book listing local treatment facilities will help you in your search. Perhaps you know someone who has experienced what you are going through. There may be someone at work who helps employees with personal problems. You will be surprised at the resources available to you.

Working with a counselor has many benefits. It is immediately helpful because you can train for and do the intervention in the counselor's office. It is critical that the intervention not be done on the chemically dependent person's "home turf", so to speak. You need a place where he cannot ask you to leave. Interventions done at home or in the chemically dependent person's office seem less effective than those done in a setting where the chemically dependent person is not quite so familiar and comfortable.

You may be able to arrange for intervention at a treatment center itself. It certainly will be easier for the chemically dependent person to stay in a treatment center after intervention than it will be for him to leave the intervention to enter treatment. In any case, it will be easier for him to enter treatment to get help for his drinking and/or using from a place where he has come to talk about your concerns around his drinking and/or using.

Most important, doing an intervention away from home territory establishes the power you as caring people have in this chemically dependent person's life from the outset. Just to get him there requires power. You will be on your own ground; he will be away from the props that give his illness confidence and power. And you want to tap every ounce of power you can muster to overpower the illness and initiate recovery.

5

Who Should Be Involved In Intervention?

You are beginning to consider forming an intervention team. This should include all the people in the chemically dependent person's life who are important to him, who have power with him, who care about him and what happens to him — all the people he will listen to.

The presence of more than one or two people is a key factor in intervention. The actual number will be determined by who really matters in this person's life and can probably range from three to thirty.

The power of intervention rests in large part on more than one person challenging the false reality the disease has created. To understand this, imagine yourself in a roomful of friends. What would happen if one person suddenly whispered to you, "You're growing a tail!" You would, of course, laugh and dismiss the observation. But if another person, and then another person, agreed, and even began to describe the tail to you, you know you would finally have to lean over your shoulder to take a peek!

This is how intervention works. One person's facts will be dismissed, but when everyone in the chemically dependent person's life is presenting a similar picture of the problems alcohol and/or drugs are creating, he will have to "take a peek".

It is important to include all members of the family at any one relationship level to the chemically dependent person. That is, if some adult brothers and sisters are part of the team, all the brothers and sisters have a place on it. Missing members can "be there" through letters or tapes, however brief. The effort put forth to secure this participation is worthwhile, for a missing member, however distant, will be spotted by the chemically dependent person and used as an invisible ally against the intervention.

It may be tempting to eliminate someone close because the chemically dependent person "hates that person". In reality, at this point the chemically dependent person may feel that he hates everybody and everybody hates him. That is one of the delusions created by the illness, and it probably should not be validated. If there is truly deep conflict between the chemically dependent person and someone in the family, it may make that person's presence on the team all the more powerful for its statement of caring.

Should The Children Be Included?

The one exception to these guidelines is the children. Although children, particularly young children, can be potent in an intervention, the risk to them is great. Often teenagers are well able to face that risk and be included as members of the team. But if you, as an adult, are apprehensive about intervention, you may be able to imagine what an overwhelming experience it might be for a very young child to confront a parent in this manner. You may choose to include young children in intervention *training*, in order to let them learn about the illness and feel part of the family effort. But someone else may speak for them in the intervention itself. They will be in the room with you through someone else's voice and words.

The team need not be limited to family members, even though they are admittedly the people with the most power in the chemically dependent person's life. There may be close friends, a minister or co-workers who also care deeply. Including such people has a distinct advantage. The chemically dependent person is less likely to rebel in the presence of "familiar strangers", and he may listen more courteously and carefully if they are there. And that, after all, is what you want. You want him to listen, really listen, to what you have to say.

The Recovering Person's Value

One final and most critical member of the intervention team is a person who is recovering from chemical dependency. Your counselor will help you find this member of your team. It may be that she/he knows people who have begun recovery through intervention and who now are willing to help others in that way. It is not necessary that you or the chemically dependent person know this man or woman. In fact, a stranger is often able to help better than a friend.

Certainly many interventions have been accomplished without a recovering team member. However, often an intervention literally turns on that unique bond of personal experience. The recovering person says, in effect, "I know how you feel because I have been there." She/he is living proof that recovery from this illness is possible. The chemically dependent person may sit quietly with arms folded and eyes downcast while you all share your concerns, only to rivet his attention on that stranger when she/he says, "I'm here, too, because I care about you, even though you don't know me. I'm a recovering alcoholic . . ."

The recovering person does not need to be involved in the initial training sessions, for that is a time for you as a family to learn and change and grow. The recovering person *must be* part of the final role play, however, so you can all be comfortable with what is about to happen. And you may find courage and strength and hope coming to you from this very special member of your team.

The one person you are not going to involve right now is the chemically dependent person. All the things you have tried before have not been successful, and now you need time to learn new and better ways to help. You need to take that time, and the chemically dependent person needs you to take it. It may feel as though you are tricking or deceiving him, sneaking behind his back to see a counselor and get information without his permission. Keep in mind that you really are sneaking behind the back of his illness, not him. And you are doing that in order to save his life.

6

How Do We Prepare For Intervention?

You are now ready to begin training for intervention. You have found a counselor and formed your team. You have some sense of what an intervention involves from the pages you have just read. It is tempting to rush to dress rehearsal, but it is here that the commitment of time, energy and emotions talked about earlier really begins.

There are definite steps in getting ready to do an intervention, and to rush any one of them is to deny yourself the chance to heal, and ultimately to deny the chemically dependent person his chance to get well.

You need to get help first because you have all become part of the illness. Out of every four people who *suffer from* chemical dependency, only one uses chemicals. The other people who suffer are called co-dependents, other victims of the illness. These people may not have a personal problem with alcohol or drugs, but because of their dealings with the chemically dependent person, they gradually become affected by his chemical use. Their feelings get changed and their behavior gets changed. Because the disease usually progresses slowly, these behavior and feeling changes happen slowly, too, and you probably haven't noticed them as they have occurred.

When the drinking or using first started, there may have been no problems. In fact, one of the first symptoms of the illness is an increase in tolerance, the ability to drink or use more and more and still continue to function. But gradually you have become aware that when the chemically dependent person and his chemical get together, bad things can happen. They don't always happen. In fact, they may have happened rarely, but you know the potential is there.

Something in your life is out of control, and you have a normal human need to control it. The chemically dependent person, by this time, also may be making sporadic attempts to control, switching brands or types of drinks or drugs, limiting times of use, changing the environment in which he uses. Because of the chronic, progressive nature of the disease, his attempts are ultimately doomed to failure, even if they seem to work temporarily.

Trying to Control

What could be more natural than for you to step in to help? You may simply have talked and reasoned with the chemically dependent person, trying to get him to cut down or stop: "Don't you think you've had enough tonight?" You may have taken the drug away from him physically — thrown it out, watered it down, hidden it. You may have tried to keep him busy with other things so he wouldn't drink and/or use. Or you may have arranged parties to limit his ability to drink and/or use.

You may have tried to keep him away from certain friends.

Sometimes these tactics work, if only for a few hours. That keeps you coming back to try again and again. But in the long run your solitary efforts are bound to fail, too. That leads to frustration and despair. But it does something else, something far more powerful. As long as he has someone else willing to control his drinking and/or using, *the chemically dependent person never really has to control it himself.*

Trying to Protect

If control won't work, then the very least you can do is try to protect the chemically dependent person from the bad things you know might happen when he drinks and/or uses. You may have begun driving so he wouldn't get hurt or hurt someone else. You may have called the job to report he had the "flu", when the drinking or using was really the cause of his sickness. You may have called a hostess the day after a party with explanations and apologies. You may have made excuses to the children, to the neighbors, to your mother-in-law, to your co-workers. You may have even bailed him out of jail, loaned him money, done his chores or work for him. You have been doing things for the chemically dependent person that are really his responsibility. At times, you may have had two jobs — being both mother and father to the children, for example.

Again, you have been normal. From the time you were small you were taught that when you love someone you protect him and care for him. After all, isn't that what your parents did for you? It feels good to care for someone, and it feels good to be cared for. But when there is a chronic, fatal illness at stake, protection and care do something else. When the chemically dependent person is rescued, when he is protected from the bad things that might happen, *the bad things never happen.*

The Enabler

If the chemically dependent person must "hit bottom", if he must face the reality of his drinking and/or using and its consequences before he gets help, then protection and control merely allow the disease to progress. That is the last thing you want to do, but out of love and devotion you have become trapped into making it easy for the chemically dependent person to continue to drink and/or use. You have become an *enabler.*

It is almost impossible to avoid doing some enabling. It is natural and normal to try to control something in your life that seems out of control, and it is only human to try to protect someone you care about. Anyone whose life touches a chemically dependent person's life probably does some enabling, totally unaware of what is happening. People at work make excuses, people at parties ignore behavior or explain it away. But unless the drinking and/or using is confronted, and confronted effectively, it will not stop. Perhaps more accurately, it cannot stop.

The Victim

When your attempts at protection and control fail, when you fix something only to have it repeat itself days or weeks or months later, something else begins to happen. One father reported feeling successful and relieved after scrambling to bail his teenage son out of jail at 2 a.m. and ensuring no charge would tarnish the young man's record. He declared, "Surely now he's learned his lesson!" Imagine his devastation when he received a repeat phone call from the same jail at 2 a.m. the next night! That father began to feel he was doing something wrong, not fixing things or protecting his son well enough. Out of frustration and confusion he began to blame himself.

No matter how hard you try, no matter what you do, things keep getting worse, because the disease keeps getting worse. But you feel that somehow it is all your fault, that somehow you are to blame, that somehow you are doing something wrong. You have become a *victim*.

The Adjuster

Finally, in desperation, you probably have just learned to put up with what is happening. You may feel, "That's just the way it is, the way it's always going to be." You know you can't really count on the chemically dependent person to carry his share of the load, so you have learned to be able to function with or without him. Most likely you have simply learned to ignore the chemically dependent person and his behavior. In order to survive, you have become an *adjuster*.

Being an *enabler* assures responsibilities will be met. Being a *victim* guarantees someone else will be blamed. And being an *adjuster* provides some relief; it allows you to go on with your life. But enabling, being a victim, and adjusting also lead you to feel angry and overwhelmed, and they allow the disease to continue.

Intervention will break all these patterns, and break them dramatically, but it will take time and effort to build toward the break.

Learning to Talk

Hopefully, you now have some rudimentary understanding that what you are facing is a disease, but you need more than a superficial knowledge of the illness. You need information and facts. It is time to educate yourselves about the enemy you are getting ready to challenge, just as any good army approaching battle would do. In the back of this book you will find a list of books and pamphlets and films that will help. Your counselor will be able to provide you with more resources. Get them. Read them. See them. Use them. Everyone on the team, not just one person, needs to do this.

Then you can begin to talk as a team. At first, you may find talking to each other difficult and painful. There are certain things you have seen the chemically dependent person do that you now can clearly recognize as symptoms of the illness. But as this illness develops some very ugly things often happen, and those probably have become secrets. Because you were ashamed, or because you didn't want to hurt or worry someone else in the family, you may not have told anyone else what you had seen or heard. Sometimes you may have even told yourself that those things really hadn't happened. Certainly you told yourself the person you care about could not really be chemically dependent.

This is the beginning of your own recovery. The chemically dependent person has been changed by the drug, and you have been changed by his use of the drug. After all, you never would have needed to keep his drinking and/or drug use a secret if he weren't drinking and/or using in such harmful and destructive ways.

All of you have been *denying*, just like the chemically dependent person. Many families say, "If we didn't talk about it, we could pretend it hadn't really happened." One wife asked her teenaged son to help her put her husband to bed after he had fallen and cut himself on the edge of a coffee table rather badly while he was drinking. They then carried the semi-conscious man upstairs and cleaned up the blood and the mess downstairs, without saying a single word to one another. Later, during intervention training, the son questioned his mother's silence during the episode. She explained, "I thought if I didn't say anything to you, you wouldn't realize what had happened."

Breaking the "Don't-Talk" Rule

That kind of behavior is normal in a family when someone is chemically dependent. You haven't been bad or sick, you've just behaved normally in the face of a very abnormal situation. But not talking about the drinking and/or using has allowed it to continue, and has added to those helpless, hopeless feelings for you, so it's time to break the *don't talk* rule.

Now that you know what chemical dependency really is — a disease with signs and symptoms, a course, and a predictable outcome if it is left untreated — you can begin to talk about it. But even using the words "alcoholic" or "chemically dependent" may be difficult.

It is rare to hear those words used rationally or factually in a family where there is chemical dependency. The words are sometimes used as insults: "You're nothing but an alcoholic!" Most families have "buzz words" for the chemical dependency: "Is Mommy 'tired' again to-night?" or "Did Daddy have a 'bad day' again today?" Everyone in the family knows what those phrases mean, but no one says the dreaded words. Now that you know what they really do mean, you can begin to use those words and use them fearlessly.

The Disease is the Enemy, Not the Person

Beginning to talk openly about what has been happening may not only be difficult. It may be frightening; it may feel like betrayal. Remember that even though it seems as if you are talking about the bad things someone you love has done, you are really talking about the bad things the disease has done to someone you love. *The disease is the enemy, not the person.*

It will help to pull an extra chair into your circle as you talk. You need to meet the missing member of your family. That chair is the drug, the disease. It is truly and equally a member of your family, as much as each of you are. It has the power to make the chemically dependent person do things and say things that he would not otherwise do or say. It has taken over the chemically dependent person's life, and in doing so it has taken over a large part of your lives. It is real, and it is there, and it is separate from all of you. When the chemically dependent person and the drug get together, bad things often happen, but the drug is not him, and he is not the drug.

One of the hardest parts of beginning to talk about the abnormal things that have been happening in your home is that you may no longer have a clear sense of what normal is. People who live with a chemically dependent person learn to accept the bizarre as normal. The chemically dependent person becomes more and more unpredictable and inconsistent as the disease develops, and inconsistency and unpredictability become normal.

You may have learned to serve dinner at 6 p.m. or at 2 a.m., depending upon when he arrives home. You may have learned not to plan parties, or not to accept invitations to go out, for fear of what might happen. You may have learned to watch what you say or to say nothing at all in order to avoid "rocking the boat". Children may have learned not to ask friends over in the evening in order to avoid feeling embarrassed. Employ-ers and co-workers may have learned to be ready to cover for the chemically dependent person at work. These things are not normal, but they have become normal. It helps to have someone else, like a counselor, to define what normal really is. And it helps to begin to look at the empty chair as the cause of what has not been normal in your lives.

Like the chemically dependent person, you have also been *defended*. Making excuses, laughing off uncom-fortable incidents, blaming other people, saying things like "Everyone else drinks or uses" — those are things the chemically dependent person is doing, and you probably have been doing them, too. Just like denial, this kind of behavior only allows the disease to continue. As you begin to be honest with one another and to trust one another, you will find it easier and easier to let go of your defenses and concentrate on the real problem, the disease.

Dealing with Delusion

Learning facts about the illness and talking about what has been happening also helps you to look at reality, at what you can do and what you can't do. Like the chemically dependent person, you have been *deluded*. The chemically dependent person believes that if only things would change in his life — if only you would stop nagging, if only the pressure from work would end — then he could "cut down", then he would "be better". You, too, may have believed that somehow you could fix things, get him to cut down or be better, if only you said the right words, if only you did the right things. Yet sometimes you did stop nagging, you did do the right things, only to see the drinking and/or using get worse.

Now you can see that none of the "if onlys" on any of your parts could ever really interrupt or change the course of a primary, progressive, chronic, fatal disease. The "if onlys" are delusion. The disease will not cure itself. Help and treatment are required.

You may still be tempted into *diverting*, just like the chemically dependent person. He may blame the divorce, or the job, or his childhood, or some other crisis or situation for his chemical dependency, and you may be tempted to agree with him. Every time that happens you can challenge that kind of thinking for each other. If divorce caused chemical dependency, then everyone who was divorced would be chemically dependent. And, let's face it, if a crisis in childhood caused chemical dependency, we'd likely all be chemically dependent! It doesn't matter why he is chemically dependent; it matters that he *is* chemically dependent, and he needs help.

Facts about the disease break denial. Honesty and trust take down defenses. Sharing reality with each other shatters delusions. Challenging the "whys" stops diversion.

As you begin to talk openly and honestly, as you begin to identify the drug as the true enemy, you will also begin to realize and then believe that this person you care about is not a bad person needing to get good; he is a sick person needing to get well. You will find yourself moving from helplessness and hopelessness to hope and a determination to give him the chance to recover that he deserves.

Learning to Feel

You have just taken an important step on your own road to recovery. You know the facts about the illness and you know what has really been happening to this person you care about. The known can never be as frightening or intimidating as the unknown. You have broken through your denial, lowered your defenses, faced your delusions, and stopped diverting. You have faced the enemy and know it for what it is — a disease that will be fatal if it is allowed to continue. You have made a decision to risk an honest and factual confrontation with that disease.

But to confront with facts alone will not be enough. To simply reel off a litany of the bad, uncomfortable things that have been happening will only serve to tighten the defenses of the chemically dependent person. He will feel attacked and accused, and even though he knows what you are saying is true, he will have to reject it in order to preserve his self-esteem and personhood. Your facts will only get through if they are tied to feelings.

Talking about feelings may be even harder than talking about facts. The chemically dependent person probably blames you at times, criticizes you at times, or withdraws from you at times. The feelings evoked by that kind of behavior, when it is repeated again and again and again, are so painful and so powerful that you have had to learn to bury them deep down inside in order to continue to function. So it's very understandable if you really don't know how you feel. You may simply be aware that you hurt, or that you are angry. Most likely you just feel numb.

It was suggested earlier that people who live with a chemically dependent person sometimes lose touch with what normal behavior is. These people can also lose touch with what normal feelings are. You have had to pretend for so long to the world and to each other that everything is "fine", that things at home are running smoothly, that you are happy and secure. You may no longer have much idea about what you even *could* feel if you allowed yourself to feel.

To help the chemically dependent person you need to touch those real feelings again. It's time to break the *don't feel* rule. It's probably not enough to ask yourself or each other how you *do* feel about the things that have been happening. You may have to ask yourselves, "If I had to guess what I feel, what would that be?" or "How do I think someone else might feel if that happened?" Again, your counselor will be able to help you recognize those feelings that have been hidden so deeply for so long, if only by suggesting to you what a normal person might feel in those circumstances. And you will begin to discover many other feelings besides anger — sadness and worry and fear and embarrassment and a real sense of loss.

Dealing With Your Anger

Some of your anger and helplessness may be dissipated now that you know the facts about the disease. However, even when you begin to recognize some other emotions, you may still be feeling very angry at the chemically dependent person or very trapped and imprisoned by him. Your relationship to the chemically dependent person may seem like love and hate mixed together. You are angry at the things he has said or done, but you also feel like his parent, needing to protect and rescue him from the bad things that might happen when he drinks and/or uses. You may have yelled and screamed at times, or given him the silent treatment, but you may also have taken car keys away so he wouldn't hurt himself or someone else, or you may have helped him to bed at night so he wouldn't fall asleep in a chair. You may have had to lock the back door at night, go to parties and school events for the children alone, pay bills he should have paid. In fact, by this time you may feel you need to watch and be ready to help almost constantly. One wife compared herself to a circus clown holding sticks with plates balanced on them in the air. Just like the clown, she knew that if she looked away for a moment, everything would come crashing down.

If you were to draw a picture of these ties, it might look something like this:

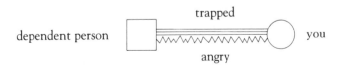

Take a look at that empty chair again. Remember that it is the drug, the disease. It is the drug that has caused the person you love to do and say those hurtful things; it is the drug that has rendered him helpless and needing your protection. In fact, your relationship really looks more like this:

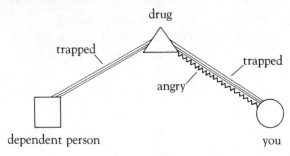

Your Anger and the Drug

As you begin to separate the chemically dependent person from the drug in your own mind, you will begin to realize that your anger and your preoccupation are really directed toward the drug. Your relationship with the chemically dependent person is now free to be filled in with feelings of love and concern.

Try expressing your anger to the chair. You will find that "I hate you" becomes "I hate what you (the drug) are doing to this person I love." "You never keep your promises to me" becomes "The drug won't let you keep your promises to me." "I always have to take care of you" becomes "When you drink or drug, the drug keeps you from doing what you want to do."

You do not have to get rid of all your feelings of anger or entrapment to do an intervention. You didn't get angry and trapped overnight, and it is hardly realistic to expect to drop those feelings after just a few sessions with a counselor and your intervention team. All you have to do is redirect those ugly feelings to the place they really belong — the disease. As you do that you will find other feelings flowing in to fill that place between you and the chemically dependent person — feelings of caring and concern and a real fear of losing this good person to the drug. These are the feelings that will get through. These are the feelings that the chemically dependent person will be able to listen to.

Writing The Script

Now that you have learned about the illness and explored with each other the things that have really been happening, now that you have identified and processed your own feelings and begun to recognize the love and concern that still remain, you are ready to plan your own intervention. It will help to view a film like *Intervention* or *I'll Quit Tomorrow*, Parts II and III, to understand firsthand what it is you are about to do. Then you can begin to write down the things you want to say to the chemically dependent person during intervention.

It is important to write for several reasons. First, an intervention is a stressful, highly emotional experience, and what seems so easy to remember in practice sessions can quickly be forgotten in the heat of the moment during intervention. Second, the chemically dependent person may object to some of the things you say during intervention, or he may try to justify himself or make excuses.

Having what you plan to say next written down will keep you from getting into a disagreement with him or being sidetracked by his defenses. Most important, the written list in front of you will let him know you are serious and mean business from the very outset.

Your counselor will begin the intervention by saying something like this: "We're all here today because everyone is concerned about what is happening to you as a result of your drinking and/or drug use. Everyone in this room has spent many hours here, learning how to help you. Your family and friends are going to share with you what they see and how they feel about that, and the things they have to say are so important they have written them down." Even if he's angry, the chemically dependent person cannot help but be impressed right away by your determination and your commitment.

You need to build your list piece by piece. When you write, start with the recent past and go back, or start in the past and move forward to the present. It is important to keep some sense of chronological order. Each person should write independently, from his or her own viewpoint. Several of you may talk about the same incident, but each of you will see it in a different perspective.

Begin by writing down what has happened, the times the drinking and/or using has caused problems or worry or concern or fear or embarrassment. Write down the times you know the chemically dependent person has tried to stop or cut down and has been unable to do so.

Avoiding Generalizations

Be specific as to time and event. If you can pinpoint dates and times, so much the better. But even "last summer" or "two Christmases ago" helps to clarify each individual incident. Avoid generalizations. Statements like "You're always drinking" or "You're never home" will be perceived as attack, and the chemically dependent person will deny their truth. In fact, he will be right. He's not *always* drinking, and he's not *always* gone, even though it may seem that way to you! He will hear you much more clearly if you say:

"Last Thursday night you came in at 2 a.m. You stumbled and knocked over a lamp."

You may be thinking, "But he knows what happened!" No, he may not, for he may be experiencing blackouts. The chemically dependent person cannot argue with *facts.*

If you reread the statement above, you can see that it seems in some ways like an accusation, a judgment that the person behaved badly. For that reason, you must tie each incident to the drinking and/or using. The chemically dependent person needs proof that he was drinking and/or using and impaired. Your statement needs to be expanded:

"Last Thursday night you came in at 2 a.m. **You had been drinking and you smelled of alcohol.** *You stumbled and knocked over a lamp.* **Your words were so slurred I had to ask you to repeat yourself."**

You may be saying to yourself, "But he knows he had been drinking heavily!" No, he may not, for the drug alters his reality. The chemically dependent person cannot argue with *evidence of drinking and/or using.*

It is important that the chemically dependent person hears what has been happening and that it has been caused by drinking and/or drug use. Facts will break through his denial and defenses. But it's much more important that he hears your feelings about what has been happening, not the feelings of anger and betrayal so much as the other feelings of love and caring and concern. To your statement you might add:

"Last Thursday night you came in at 2 a.m. You had been drinking and you smelled of alcohol. You stumbled

and knocked over a lamp. Your words were so slurred I had to ask you to repeat yourself. **I was embarrassed for you because the children heard you, and I was sad because we couldn't talk. I'm afraid I'm losing you."**

The chemically dependent person cannot argue with *your feelings.*

Finally, you need to talk about the good qualities you know this person possesses, the good things you know you can share. It may not be enough to begin by saying, "I'm here because I care about you," and then follow that with a list of only facts and feelings. By the time the illness has progressed this far the chemically dependent person probably feels very worthless inside. Remember he doesn't yet understand the disease as you do. So your final statement might sound something like this:

"I remember when we were first married how I used to look forward to your coming home so we could talk. We used to tell each other that the time we spent together meant so much to both of us. Sometimes it is still like that. You listen to me and I feel you care. But last Thursday night you came in at 2 a.m. You had been drinking and you smelled of alcohol. You stumbled and knocked over a lamp. Your words were so slurred I had to ask you to repeat yourself. I was embarrassed for you because the children heard you, and I was sad because we couldn't talk. I'm afraid I'm losing you."

The chemically dependent person cannot argue with *what you believe is good about him.*

Each individual incident on your list needs to be developed in this fashion. You may want to share some of what you have learned in intervention training to identify the disease as the enemy more clearly. For example:

"Last February you promised me you would stop drinking. I know you meant that promise and I believed you. You didn't have anything to drink for two weeks, and I was so proud of you. But then we went to the office party. You said you'd only have one, and I know you intended to do that. Instead, you had five or six drinks before dinner and we had to leave the party early. I was embarrassed and disappointed, and I know you were, too. But I've learned here that it wasn't your fault. I've learned that what is happening to you is a disease you can't control and I can't control. I know you need help."

Team members who are not so close to the chemically dependent person will probably not possess such specific details about the drinking and/or drug use and its consequences. They can point out their concerns in a more general way:

"You used to drop over and visit me several times a week, and I looked forward to seeing you. But you haven't come over at all for the past four months. Now you seem to be avoiding me, as though something else is more important in your life. From what other people have said here, I think your drinking may be the reason you don't stop to see me anymore. Looking back, I remember that when I didn't offer you a beer right away, you would make an excuse to leave pretty quickly after you arrived. You are a good friend to me and I miss you. I agree that you need help."

Your list will present the chemically dependent person with evidence of what drinking and/or drug use has been doing to him. It will separate him from his disease before his very eyes.What has been happening is not his fault; it is not anybody's fault. The disease is to blame. He has tried and tried hard. He has not failed; the disease has failed you all. Your list will also let him know how much you care and want him back. And it will convince him that he is worth the effort, that he is worth recovery.

Dress Rehearsal

Now it's time to practice together what you will say in intervention. Your counselor will introduce why you are here and what you will be talking about. Your counselor will also secure an agreement from the chemically dependent person that he will listen to what you all have to say before he talks. The first person on the team to speak should be someone who has not only clear facts about the drinking and/or using but also real power with the chemically dependent person, someone the chemically dependent person is most likely to listen to without interruption. Often this is not a member of the family, but that "familiar stranger", an in-law, a good friend, a minister or a co-worker. As you establish the order in which you will speak you can build on that opening power.

There may be people on the team who have less intimate knowledge about the drinking and/or using than others. They should speak after the existence of a problem has been clearly established with facts.

There may be someone on the team whose relationship to the chemically dependent person has been fraught with conflict, that "person he hates" mentioned earlier. That person should also be placed in the middle of the sequence. In order to avoid arousing hostility, it may be that this "enemy" says no more than "I care about you, and I hope you will listen to what everyone else has to say."

Tapes and letters from missing family members need to be placed in order, and how you will share them needs to be practiced. If someone is going to talk for very young children, that role must be integrated into the flow of the intervention.

Dress rehearsal is also a time to gently eliminate anyone on the team who is not yet comfortable with the idea of intervention, anyone who might be less than helpful. But since you cannot know who or what will ultimately be the catalyst in the intervention, you may be willing to coach that reluctant team member just a bit further.

Learning To Trust

Although no intervention is likely to be carried out word for word as it is rehearsed, it's important that each of you knows what the others plan to say, so there are no big surprises on intervention day. Even though you have already talked together openly and honestly, you may still find some new information being shared at final role play. You have learned over the years that you cannot trust one of the most important people in your life — the chemically dependent person. Your trust in each other has eroded as a result of that. Today is the day to finally break the *don't trust* rule, and that is the rule that crumbles most slowly.

Being Prepared

You can help each other avoid using four words that will be red flags to the chemically dependent person — "drunk", "chemically dependent", "alcoholic", and "treatment". The chemically dependent person will object to being called drunk. The drug has deluded him, and his perception of himself as being in control will argue with that "drunk" judgment. It's not critical that he knows he was drunk. "You had been drinking" or "You had so much to drink" will establish equally that the drug is the villain.

You also are not out to diagnose this person alcoholic or chemically dependent, even though you now firmly believe he is. That is a conclusion he must reach himself with the help of treatment, for that self-diagnosis is an integral step in the recovery process. All you need establish in intervention is that "drinking and/or drug use is causing a problem for you."

Finally, if anyone in the initial sharing at intervention mentions the word treatment, the chemically dependent person may be distracted by that: "What do they mean by treatment?" He may not be able to listen to the rest of what you have to say. It is better to suggest only that "You need help." After you have finished sharing your fact lists and presenting convincing proof that there is a problem, the counselor will describe treatment, and the recovering member of your team will be there to offer hope and personal witness to its rewards.

Practice sharing your lists in order without interrupting each other, for any interruption will dilute the power of the person speaking and divert the chemically dependent person's attention. It is helpful to have someone present at final role play to pretend to be the chemically dependent person. This gives you a chance to practice handling any interruptions or objections he is likely to provide.

As you rehearse you may find tears beginning to fall. You may fear you cannot get through what you have to say without crying. Those tears are real and they are powerful, and you may cry during intervention. So may the chemically dependent person. Practice taking a deep breath and continuing to share. You have already learned you can have real and deep feelings, and you can show them to each other. This is a time for helping each other and for bonding. You are coming together, gaining strength from one another, becoming a team powerful enough to overpower the disease.

Planning Treatment

Dress rehearsal is a time to establish final treatment options. What will you ask the chemically dependent person to do in order to get well? Will he enter an inpatient or outpatient treatment program, see a counselor, go to support groups like A.A.? Your counselor will help you suggest the best treatment plan based on the history and progression of the illness and what is available in your community. The counselor in this instance is an agent for you, the family, not an agent for the treatment center, even though she/he may be employed there. You will have a "first and best" treatment plan in mind, which may include admission to a program at the facility where the intervention is taking place. However, you may want to make tentative arrangements for more than one treatment option, to allow for some flexibility. You will certainly want to visit first the place or places you are asking the chemically dependent person to go to for help.

Final role play is also the time to establish consequences. What will you do if the chemically dependent person refuses to get help? Consequences must be enforceable and able to be enforced immediately. You may have to continue to carry them out over a period of time. There have been too many empty threats and broken promises for everyone over the course of the years.

Unless you have bags packed and a place to stay that night, it is probably unwise to threaten to leave. It might be more realistic to say, "I don't know how much longer I can go on with you like this." Adult children who are the parents of grandchildren may want to refuse to let the chemically dependent person see those grandchildren. Admittedly, that is a powerful consequence, but one that might be difficult or impossible to enforce at holiday times. Perhaps it would be more manageable to promise, "We will not let the grandchildren ride with you in the car when you are driving," or "We will not let you babysit for the grandchildren when you are alone." Co-workers may be tempted to threaten termination. Unless that is to be done on intervention day, it will probably be more realistic to state, "I will not cover up for you at work any longer."

The most powerful consequence you all have is your own commitment to continue recovery yourselves. You promise yourselves and the chemically dependent person that you will go on and get well — with or without him. You will continue education and counseling and attend Al-Anon. You will not suffer from his illness any longer. You will no longer support his being sick. You will no longer protect and rescue him from the consequences of his disease. You will no longer enable, be a victim or adjust. Now you will support only recovery.

In reality, you can back the chemically dependent person into a corner with enough threats and consequences so that there is no choice for him but to enter treatment. But it is difficult to begin recovery flattened against a wall. Rather, you want to love this person into treatment. You want to help him separate himself from his disease and join with him to overpower that illness. You want to convince him that he is a good person who is worth recovery and deserves no less. It is now time to give him permission to lead you all into recovery, and the choice is his.

7

When Are We Ready For Intervention?

Not until all this is done are you ready to schedule intervention. It is natural to concentrate on the goal of intervention itself, on that overwhelming moment when the chemically dependent person enters a roomful of the most important and significant people in his life and you begin the confrontation that hopefully will lead to treatment. But perhaps you already are beginning to see that intervention is a gradual process, not just a one-time event.

You as a family, a team of caring people, have changed gradually through intervention training. Even if you have said nothing in words to the chemically dependent person about the counseling you have been getting and the preparations you have been making, you cannot help but have changed. You have new knowledge and a new sense of determination and hope. Do not be surprised if you find that change transmitted unwittingly to the chemically dependent person. It is not uncommon for the chemically dependent person to alter his drinking and/or using pattern in some way during this period of time. He may drink and/or use more, or he may try to cut down or even attempt to quit.

With your counselor you will want to prepare and outline the steps you will take to use any potential crisis positively to initiate treatment if the drinking and/or using escalates during intervention training. If the chemically dependent person makes an attempt to control his drinking and/or using, you may be tempted to back away from intervention. You know too much now to be fooled by such changes; you know they reflect the illness itself fighting desperately for its very survival. You may have seen earlier such efforts end in failure and despair. Now is the time to continue.

You need to work together to plan answers for all the chemically dependent person's objections to treatment. Make arrangements for child care, if those are necessary. Have some idea as to how responsibilities at work will be handled. If no one at the chemically dependent person's place of employment knows about the intervention effort, remember that if he broke his leg today, he would be in the hospital today, and the job responsibilities would be covered. You believe this disease is just that serious, and that treatment, immediate treatment, is just that essential.

Know how treatment is to be paid for and arrange for a bed at a treatment center if that is your recommendation. You may even bring a packed suitcase to intervention. You will probably be asking the chemically dependent person to go directly from intervention into treatment, for it is easiest and most effective for all of you to seize the magic moment when he agrees that he needs help. At the very least, set a firm date and time for treatment to begin.

Standing Firm

Be prepared to let nothing stand in the way of your request. That is the hardest part of intervention, hanging on until that agreement for treatment is reached. It is likely you will get the chemically dependent person to concede that there is a problem, but he may want to take care of it "on his own". You have evidence that his solitary efforts in the past have been unsuccessful. He may even agree that he needs help. But he may want to get help "tomorrow". You know now that the defenses will come back quickly, that the disease will fight to keep him sick, and tomorrow may never come. You want and deserve a firm commitment to treatment today before he leaves the room.

Handling the Intervention Invitation

To get the chemically dependent person to intervention itself one member of the team, usually the closest person, will do a mini-intervention. If you are the one chosen for this role, approach the chemically dependent person at a time when he is not drinking and/or using, preferably the morning after a night of heavy use when he may be feeling remorseful and will be more open to listening. Share with him your concern about the drinking and/or using. Tell him you have been to see a counselor and ask that he come with you to talk to the counselor just once. You may have to mention some of the facts you plan to use in intervention in order to convince him that he needs to come. You will repeat those facts again in front of everyone during intervention.

It is critical that the chemically dependent person be tricked as little as possible at this point. If he thinks he is coming to see a marriage counselor, or to attend a business meeting, he may feel so deceived and manipulated when he realizes what intervention is really all about that he will be unable to listen to what you have to say. He needs to know he is coming to talk to someone about his drinking and/or using. All he will not know is who else is to be there.

Be firm and determined not to take "no" for an answer. After all that has happened, this is the least he can do. Remember, all you are asking for is an hour of his time. All you are asking is that he come to see a counselor once. What happens as a result of that session will be his choice.

It is possible that the chemically dependent person may resist even this small step. In that case the intervention can be done in stages. You may need to wait until the next crisis occurs before you approach him again with your request that he see a counselor. Or several team members may have to make the initial approach together. Some families have carried out an entire intervention at home simply to get the chemically dependent person to agree to see a counselor and then have repeated the intervention in the counselor's office to secure an agreement for treatment.

However, the chemically dependent person will likely agree to see this counselor with you. He will probably come out of curiosity, to find out who has been giving you information, and to tell his side of the story. He may believe he can fool the counselor, for he has fooled everyone else for as long as he can remember.

Team Power

But he will walk in on the combined power of a caring family, the power of a prepared team. That power cannot be underestimated. And it can work. It can work even if the team does not quite believe in its own power. The chemically dependent person may walk in angry, like the man who took one look at the intervention team assembled before him and asked, "What did you all get — thirty pieces of silver?" That man now helps with other interventions. He may walk in prepared, like the woman who brought along her own written list of her family's faults and then quietly folded that up without reading it as she agreed to treatment.

It may be possible to brush off one person who cares and dismiss that person from a life, but it is virtually impossible to turn away from everyone who matters. Beyond that, there is a real and good person underneath all that bravado and anger and isolation, a person who desperately wants not to be this way, a person who wants all of this to end. The power of your love will let him reach inside himself to tap the part of himself that really does want to get well.

Intervention is a risk, a real and significant risk. You may fear anger and rejection from the chemically dependent person. You may be jeopardizing friendship, love, even financial stability. Intervention takes powerful love and incredible courage. But intervention is a shared risk, and your love and courage are augmented by your power as a team.

What you have been doing in intervention training is redefining love. You have learned that all the old ways of loving and caring are not so helpful when a chronic, fatal illness is involved. Now you have decided to love the chemically dependent person enough to take a monumental risk. You are willing to face the unknown, to shake your own complacency and security, in order to give him the chance to recover.

8

Some Final Thoughts

No intervention ever fails. Even if treatment is refused you have planted a seed that may bear fruit weeks or months from now. And you will continue to intervene, gently and caringly, with your new knowledge and skills. If the drinking and/or using continues, you will continue to confront it, renewing your offer of help. You will carry out the consequences you established in intervention. In other words, you will withdraw your support from the illness, but you will keep supporting the person you care about.

Beyond that, you as a family and you as a team have changed and changed irrevocably. You have broken long-established rules. You have talked and shared feelings and supported and trusted one another, and you have begun to heal. You have met the enemy and know it for a disease that is not your fault, not anybody's fault. You are no longer helpless and hopeless and full of despair. You know there is help for you and for the chemically dependent person. You know that recovery is possible. You will never be the same.

An intervention, well-planned and well-prepared for, is worth the effort for everyone, no matter what the immediate results seem to be. Yes, it is an effective tool for motivating the chemically dependent person into treatment. More important, you now know you have done everything. Your decisions from now on can be based on love and reality, not in anger and a need for revenge.

And as you keep your commitment to yourself to go on and get well — as you withdraw your support from the disease, as you cease your preoccupation with what the chemically dependent person is doing and channel your energies into your own growth and change — you will begin to find the peace and serenity that healing brings. Ultimately, the chemically dependent person may have no choice but to follow you on the journey to recovery.

Part II

To The Therapist

Beginning Perceptions

A family that suffers from chemical dependency is strong and courageous and loving. Their strength and courage and love reach deep into the core of their being and bond them with ties an ordinary family can scarcely imagine much less imitate. This is a family that has weathered crisis after crisis and stayed connected; this is a family that has felt pain and hurt beyond belief and repressed that pain and hurt in order to survive; this is a family that has kept up appearances and maintained some semblance of ritual and continuity against all odds. The members of this family have learned incredible skills and possess sophisticated coping mechanisms — their very existence bears mute testimony to their talents.

Such a description is likely anathema to most counselors who work with chemically dependent families. But it may be a mistake to label this family "weak" or "nonfunctional". In fact, they have functioned with minimal apparent disturbance within the parameters of their disturbed circumstances. They have responded normally to abnormality; they have adapted to the unadaptable. They may have endured in a crippled, sometimes dysfunctional and pathological state, *but they have continued to endure.* They may have communicated in destructive and damaging ways, *but they have continued to communicate.*

It is not that they lack strength or love or bonds; it is that their strength and love and bonds have been warped and corroded by the disease in their midst. Therapy with this family is not a matter of building strengths and bonds from nothing or creating love where none is present; it is rather a matter of redirecting and restructuring their existing strength and love and bonds into new, more helpful and more useful pathways. Indeed, we might do well to eliminate the words "sick" and "well" from our vocabularies before we approach this family. Phrases like "not useful" and "useful", "less helpful" and "more helpful", are more realistic and more accurate and more therapeutic descriptions for them and for us. These words are more accurate and realistic because the behavior and patterns family members have developed have allowed them all to get to this point. From a primitive perspective they have kept themselves and the chemically dependent person alive. These words are more therapeutic because to tell these people that they are sick is to alienate them at the outset. They see reality in this regard better than we do — they know they have coped and they know they have survived.

We need to approach this family with a sense of wonder at the pain and struggle they will be willing to expose to us and the growth we will be permitted to share with them. Their recovery will not be a diametric shift from sick to well; rather it will be a gradual transition of skills already in place from less useful and less helpful to more useful and more helpful.

We will tap the courage they have needed to stand against adversity and keep the world away, but we will urge them to use that courage to face the fearful and unknown instead. We will mobilize the strength they have developed to endure pain and hurt, but we will teach them to use that strength to confront the disease and their own denial. We will ask them to love, not to maintain the destructive status quo, but to change it, to risk what tenuous security and stability they have managed to maintain in order to save one of their own.

Intervention is a process, not an event. Our task as therapists is to intervene on the family, to lead the family away from denial and delusion into reality and recovery. But before that can be done we must refocus ourselves: the first intervention is with the intervention counselor. We must clear away our own issues and prejudices and our own hidden agendas about chemical dependency and the chemically dependent family. In that regard, some of us may need to deal with the wreckages of our own pasts. We need to come before this family with a clear understanding and acceptance of chemical dependency as a disease and a firm conviction that the family did not cause the disease but rather that the disease caused the family.

The Continuum of Family Recovery

Intervention is a strategy, just one tool among several, that can be used to affect recovery for the chemically dependent family. Whatever the method, recovery for the chemically dependent family progresses along a continuum that begins with the therapist and becomes an ongoing evolution toward serenity and genesis for the family. Treatment and recovery for the chemically dependent family member follow as the natural outcome of that metamorphosis.

Stage One — Refocusing

For a period of time we as therapists are going to become members of this family. The definition of family for this purpose is the intervention team, all those people in the chemically dependent person's life who care about him and are concerned about him, all those people whose behavior and feelings have in some way been affected or changed by his drinking and/or using.

At the beginning we may be the only realistic, rational family member. But we must meet this family on its own terms and enter them exactly where they are — denying, deluded, defended and diverting. We will refuse to become part of their maladaptive system. Our skills and knowledge as therapists will keep us from falling prey to their denial, delusion, defenses and diversion. Rather, we will become catalysts and role models for change and for refocus. We will lead the family out of their delusion and denial and into reality; we will direct their attention away from the defensive and distracting chimeras of their guilt and rationalization and projection and onto the substance of the disease.

Before this process can even begin some modicum of trust must be established. This is an obvious given in any therapeutic relationship, but the issues for this family are deeper and more intense. One of their operative rules is *don't trust*. They don't even trust each other; their willingness to trust an outsider is less than zero. Their trust has eroded over years of unpredictability and inconsistency, and that is how trust must be built, with consistency and predictability. The implications for the therapist begin with the first phone call, and we need to be there for this family to support them from the beginning, both at a basic and at a more sophisticated level.

Family Characteristics

This is not a family that will respond nonchalantly to changed appointment times or locales. Their surface patina may insist that anything is acceptable to them, but any vacillation will reaffirm their underlying conviction that nothing or no one can be counted on. These are people to whom promises made must be promises kept. Ideally, we need to be there for them when and where we promise; it even makes sense to work with this family in the same room from beginning to end if that is possible. If anyone is to be inconvenienced, better the therapist than the family. This is obviously a family that will be devastated by any change in counselors. Rotating training sessions among colleagues may be efficient from the therapist's or facility's point of view, but it will likely alienate the family and force them to withdraw, frustrating any attempts at progress.

When we understand the entry level family dynamics, it becomes apparent that both the family's and the therapist's interests are best served by consistency. This takes an unusual degree of dedication from a counselor and a unique kind of backing from a facility or corporate administration, but it is worth fighting for and committing to at the outset.

The refocusing stage of family treatment is, at a basic level, educational. It is not enough to assume that the family knows there is a problem and is ready to proceed with intervention simply because they have presented themselves for training. They have come out of desperation and helplessness, and it is rare to find more than one or two people in the entire family group more than minimally convinced that intervention is truly necessary or possible. In fact, most family members are so reluctant to break from this position of hopelessness that we ask the person who initially contacts us to approach significant others, not with the idea of intervention, but rather with a request to "come talk to a counselor just once to see if there is some way we as a family can help". It is up to us as counselors to sell the family on intervention and on their own power.

Dealing With The Faulty Belief System

It is helpful to begin immediately to supply facts about the disease and the drug, with didactic information or with films like *The Disease Concept of Alcoholism* or *Drug Dependency*. But understanding the delusional, diversionary reality of the family, understanding they really are convinced that they are somehow to blame for what has been happening, leads us to know that direct confrontation will not be helpful. It is not enough to label as false and dismiss out of hand the cognitive system they have lived with for so long. That simply will not be credible to them. We need to listen to and acknowledge the reasons and explanations they have supplied and accepted, and then we can begin to challenge gently and specifically the pieces of self-blame and excuses one by one.

The faulty belief system that has held them all in thrall can be penetrated with variations of rational emotive or reality therapy techniques. For example, if heavy drinking and/or using friends caused chemical dependency, then everyone who had heavy drinking and/or using friends would be chemically dependent. Yet they all have a chemically dependent "friend" — the person they care about — and they are not chemically dependent. If life problems caused chemical dependency, then everyone who had problems in life would be chemically dependent. Soon the family will begin to challenge their own delusions and diversion for themselves.

At this point we also begin to role model a rational, factual approach to the disease in order to dissolve the family's denial and defenses. We are people who will not "go crazy" when the words "alcoholic" or "chemically dependent" are mentioned or when drinking and/or using "craziness" is discussed. Instead, we begin to redefine the terrible, embarrassing, even disgusting events they have witnessed not as signs of bad behavior or weak personality but as symptoms of an illness.

Dealing With The Disease

This is the time to introduce the empty chair as the disease. That chair will continue to be present in all our ensuing sessions with the family. It will take on new life and meaning as therapy progresses. For now, it is a tool to separate the chemically dependent person from the drug and to introduce reality at an intellectual level; it is a tool to permit rational discussion of disease rather than judgmental accusations about will power and self control. As long as the family believes that what has been happening is shameful and somehow their fault, that their history is a revelation of bad personality or bad family, they will have to continue their denial and defend against outside intrusion. When we separate the disease from them and from the chemically dependent person, they can lower their defenses and discard their denial. They can begin to break the *don't talk* rule on a factual level.

It may be comfortable and affirming to describe ourselves as therapists. But therapy with the chemically dependent family cannot start until we have first educated and then role modelled. If the thrust of therapy is to change this family, then we had better be certain we educate them so that they understand why they *need* to change before we ask them to change. And we had better be sure we show them how they *can* change before we ask them to change.

As the walls of silence begin to crumble, as the family becomes more comfortable talking about what has been happening as symptomatic of disease, rather than indicative of something terribly wrong about them, they will become more willing to open themselves to the world around them. They will no longer need to retreat and hide in their attempts to conceal their anguish. At this point they may reveal other people who could help the intervention effort, and they may become more amenable to involving extended family members who have been excluded until now. Although the education phase may need to be lengthened or repeated to insure that newcomers become equal and functional team members, it is well worth the time and energy required.

Refocusing sets the stage for altered behavior and feelings. It accepts the family at the level of their diversionary and deluded perception of reality and redefines those perceptions with empirical knowledge and a model and rationale for change. It establishes the possibility for trust and consistency and begins to break down the defensiveness and denial that have dominated their existence as a family for so long. It is ignorance and delusion that keep the *don't talk* rule in place, and it is the knowledge and reality provided by refocusing that breaks the *don't talk* rule.

Stage Two — Reframing

Having redefined reality for the family, it is time to redefine the family itself. Up until now the chemically dependent person has been the most powerful member of the family because he has been inextricably linked to his drug. It has been the unpredictable and inconsistent behavior caused by the drug that has led the family to react and overreact to the chemically dependent person, to tiptoe around him so as not to "rock the boat", to avoid him or even to fear him.

Now that the family has some basic understanding of the disease, now that the drug has been disjoined from the chemically dependent person, the family can approach each of them independently. In structural family therapy terms, this is the phase of empowerment. The division of the enemy, new knowledge about the nature of the enemy, and the combined presence of the family allow empowerment at three different levels. The family now knows what it is that they are dealing with. They see the drug weakened by its separation from the chemically dependent person. They know they outnumber whatever force it can muster. The disease becomes for them a "thing", an entity, not a person. They are people, and people are more powerful than things. But it is not enough to talk about the family's new power. Their power must be visually reinforced for them by their literal encirclement of that empty chair.

Separation of the chemically dependent person from the drug also allows the family to rebond in different ways. As their anger and frustration are directed at the disease, at the empty chair, they can cease their destructive blaming toward the chemically dependent person and toward each other. As their feelings of entrapment are tied to the empty chair, they can loosen the stranglehold they have felt coming from the chemically dependent person himself.

This allows them to ally themselves with the chemically dependent person against the disease, even without the presence of the chemically dependent person. He again becomes part of the family, first in their imaginations and then in fact. They will convey this new alliance to the chemically dependent person during the intervention, offering him a part of their own newly developed power to break from his disease.

The structural reframing of the family around the disease/empty chair not only validates and empowers the family; it allows this process to occur quickly and effectively. Certainly full recovery for this family requires them to acknowledge and work through all the uncomfortable and painful feelings the disease has engendered, but to insist that they do this through emotional exploration and verbal probing may be to sentence them to a lifetime of therapy. Most of us as therapists do not have months or years to work with this family. Reframing offers speed. The entire intervention training process can be accomplished in eight to twelve hours of concentrated effort if reframing is utilized.

The family may continue to experience their painful feelings, but if those feelings are redirected toward the disease, rather than the chemically dependent person, the family may be able to save a life in the course of their own healing. The impact of that watershed experience on their own progress cannot be measured. At the very least, reframing allows them to reach the turning point of intervention, with its concomitant knowledge and assurance that they have done all that they can. That catharsis may best provide the freedom and release necessary to catalyze true family recovery.

The Importance of Speed

And if intervention is the chosen course of action for the family, we owe them all the speed we can effect. Hanging on and enduring during the active illness is agonizing enough; the tension and suspense a family undergoes during the drive toward intervention, as that light at the end of the tunnel beckons them, is almost unbearable. Families liken the days before intervention to waiting for the surgeon's knife or the executioner's axe to fall. Surely we must do everything we can to ease their burden.

Beyond empowerment and speed, however, the most important result of reframing, in terms of family recovery, lies in the release of feelings. When the disease is defined as a separate entity, all the feelings that have been so long directed toward the chemically dependent person can now flow toward the disease that has really triggered them. There is much guilt evoked by admitting hate toward a parent or a spouse or a child; there can be no guilt about hating a disease. There is much shame attached to being embarrassed or disgusted by a parent or a spouse or a child; there can be no shame in being embarrassed or disgusted by a disease. Feelings that have lain dormant for years, festering and simmering under the surface, can begin to be admitted and touched and experienced and resolved. It is guilt and shame that keep the *don't feel* rule in place, and it is freeing and exploring feelings through reframing that break the *don't feel* rule.

Stage Three — Redirecting

Once the family has a clear sense of their own reality, once they have lowered their defenses to confront and demolish the denial and delusion they have been living with, once they are focused on the disease rather than their own diversions, the energy they have been devoting to containing the disease and hiding their own feelings will be liberated. This new energy is expressed as love and concern and caring, not only for the chemically dependent person but for each other. This energy then needs to be directed into ongoing recovery for them.

This is the stage at which a final decision about intervention should be reached. Intervention may be high drama, but it is not a play with set lines and a guaranteed happy ending. The choice to proceed with intervention should not be made lightly, for intervention is a powerful tool not to be used carelessly or precipitously.

There may be a multiplicity of immediate and long-range considerations — the chemically dependent person's medical or emotional status, possible unacceptable social or financial ramifications, the stage and progression of the disease — that argue against intervention. The family itself must also be considered. Even if some family members are motivated and enthusiastic about intervention, the whole team must be convinced that intervention is the best and only option. If one significant person is not involved, or is present only "on the sidelines", the intervention stands less chance of success. In fact, if that is the case, intervention may not only push the chemically dependent person deeper into his defenses and his disease; it may also fragment and factionalize the family with blame and guilt that will block their recovery, send them back into a worsening spiral of denial and dysfunction, and perpetuate their agony.

Family Recovery

One of the hardest parts of intervention training is to guide the family away from intervention and to direct their newly discovered and unleashed energy and love and caring solely toward themselves and their own recovery. This will violate all that they have focused on and hoped for; it will reawaken fear and helplessness and hopelessness, and they will need tremendous support and encouragement to forge ahead to recovery and not regress.

If intervention is the chosen option, then it, too, becomes the cornerstone for family recovery. The family is led to take this risk for themselves more than for the chemically dependent person. They are venturing into uncertainty and upheaval to reach the peace and freedom that lie on the other side of the chasm. They are doing this to assure themselves that they have taken every step possible. They are doing this to lay open what has been secret and hidden, to unshackle themselves from the chains of the disease.

Freeing the chemically dependent person may also result, but their first goal is to free themselves, to simply and honestly love and care. Their energy will flow into bonding and sharing. It is fear and hopelessness that keep the *don't trust* rule in place, and it is redirecting energy into faith and love that finally begins to topple the *don't trust* rule that started to be shaken at the outset. It will probably take final role play to batter down the *don't trust* rule completely.

Stage Four — Reinforcement

Even when the decision to intervene is irrevocable, there is still a need for consolidation. This is the time for the "housekeeping" of intervention — choosing the treatment facility and treatment modality, booking the bed, arranging for child care and employment coverage. This is also the time to decide the identity of the recovering person who will share intervention with the family. That choice needs to be made by the counselor with the full knowledge of the family and the optimal understanding of the chemically dependent person, which can only be achieved after all the family rules have been broken, after all the secrecy has been unveiled. Although any recovering person may be helpful, a recovering person whose history is compatible with the chemically dependent person's and whose personality is complementary to the family will offer strength and hope to the team beyond the framework of simple identification.

This period of time also provides an opportunity for elimination of any team member who may be counter-productive. The team can cope with the shock of losing one of their members best when they are fully bonded. Elimination of a team member should be a last resort, however, for the risk of weakening or destroying the team is great. It is probably better to modify the structure of the intervention and the participation of that particular team member, perhaps by placing him/her in a middle position with less clout in the order of the intervention or by editing what she/he is going to say, rather than to completely cast away a part of the team.

The time for making final arrangements for intervention and treatment is also the time for clearing away any lingering doubts on the family's part. It is now, just as the family's determination becomes most solid, that the chemically dependent person is likely to react to the incipient recovery he senses in the family by making an attempt to change his drinking and/or using pattern. This alteration of behavior in the chemically dependent person, like the shift in the family's approach to him, probably takes place below the level of consciousness, because it often occurs while the family is insisting that they have done nothing to disrupt the precarious balance. But their new knowledge and their new sense of purpose all but insure a lessening of scorn and self-deprecation, a dissolution of helplessness and desperation, and a growing resolve. These are monumental innuendos that vibrate through the gridlock in which the chemically dependent person has heretofore held sway.

Sometimes the ensuing stress is used to justify an increase in drinking and/or using that precipitates a crisis for the chemically dependent person. The family must be prepared to initiate treatment on an emergency basis in that eventuality. More frequently, the chemically dependent person's undeliberated response will be to cut down or even quit using the chemical altogether. At this point the family will be tempted to bolt — all their old doubts will resurface. It may be necessary to retrace the entire course of the illness with the family to assure them that the present improvement is only a brief hiatus, a momentary aberration in the inexorable progression of the disease.

From an ethical and humanitarian standpoint, it would seem best not to schedule final role play until this last hurdle has been cleared. To take a family through final role play without a definite assurance that intervention will follow almost immediately seems unnecessarily cruel. In all but the most unusual cases, it is imperative that an agreement that the chemically dependent person will come to see the counselor for the intervention session be secured before final role play is accomplished. The adrenalin and energy set in motion at dress rehearsal need the release that probably only intervention itself can effect.

Unpredictable Role Play

No final role play, like no intervention, is ever predictable. The family that has held onto vestiges of guardedness and secrecy may open totally at this penultimate experience, while the family that has seemed so ready and disclosive may balk and withdraw in discomfort at the pretense and forced emotion of the rehearsal. It seems impossible to predict the character the intervention will take from the final role play. Each family needs to prepare and gather its forces for intervention in its own particular style. Some families will work and rework their fact lists together; others will skate through their presentations superficially and apologetically. But each in their own way, they will cry and laugh together and support one another.

Final role play should not necessarily be viewed as a word by word rehearsal. Rather, it is simply the family's final opportunity to bond and heal before they go into battle to face the disease, and they can be allowed to undertake that task in the manner most comfortable for them.

Final role play may be unpredictable in other, unexpected ways. Because of the emotion generated, this is often the session during which a chemically dependent team member self-identifies and asks for help for him/herself. As therapists we may have suspected the presence of the disease in that team member from the beginning, but part of the contract, so to speak, between team and therapist is that team members' chemical use is not an issue. They are present on the team to help the identified chemically dependent person because they care about him. However, the impact of factual education and the introduction of safe, caring surroundings supportive of recovery cannot be underestimated; the team's shared love and concern can be an overwhelming catalyst for recovery in one of their own.

If our goal in intervention training is to heal the family, then chemical dependency treatment for that affected team member is part of personal healing. It is prudent to anticipate a cry for help from a team member and to be prepared to facilitate possible treatment for him/her before the actual intervention, at a time when it does not fragment and distract from the primary intervention effort.

Stage Five — Recovery

If we are working with the family along their own continuum of recovery, we will not see intervention as the end of our effort, and we will not abandon the family after intervention even if they believe they have achieved their goal. This is the time they may need us most. No matter whether the chemically dependent person has entered treatment or refused help, the family is still just beginning. The four stages which have gone before — refocusing, reframing, redirecting and reinforcement — these have merely brought them to the threshold of their own recovery, and they will need to be nudged onward.

It seems a mistake to agree to work toward intervention with a family unless they are willing to make a firm commitment to continuing recovery for themselves. This commitment can take many shapes and forms, varying according to their individual needs and their degree of closeness to the chemically dependent person, but it must be present. Otherwise, intervention becomes simply an "instant fix" that implies that the chemically dependent person is the only one who needs to get well. But no matter how solid the earlier agreement for ongoing family treatment has been, the family will still need encouragement to persevere.

Following Intervention

At the very least each team deserves a final session with the counselor to process the intervention, whether it succeeded or whether it failed. They may need close and continual support during the hours and days following intervention, as the chemically dependent person begins to deal with the anger and shame surrounding the intervention either in a treatment setting or outside. All the old doubts will resurface: "Did we over-react?" "Did we do the right thing?" "Will he ever forgive us?"

Hopefully, if all has gone well, the family will be involved in a formal family treatment program within the confines of the treatment facility where the chemically dependent person is getting help. If not, they may need to be referred to family treatment on an outpatient basis.

Now is also the time to introduce them to the lifetime support systems of Al-Anon and Alateen, a referral that was not appropriate during formal intervention training. Intervention may be compatible with the Al-Anon philosophy at a theoretical and intellectual level: reduced to the simplistic, Al-Anon teaches the family to allow the chemically dependent person to suffer the natural consequences of his drinking and/or drug use, and certainly one of the most obvious natural consequences of dependent drinking and/or drug use is that someone will talk to the chemically dependent person about it. In fact, intervention is a compilation and cataloging of all the events and consequences that have occurred.

However, Al-Anon and intervention training juxtaposed are much too confusing for the family. Al-Anon's message that active drinking and/or using can be tolerated and accepted with peace and serenity until a natural crisis occurs seems to contradict intervention's plan that the family interrupt the course of the illness by creating a managed crisis. It is not until intervention is accomplished, whatever the result, that Al-Anon becomes truly meaningful and helpful for this particular family.

Techniques and Strategies

Working with a chemically dependent family calls upon all the skills and knowledge we possess as therapists and then some. We are more often required to intuitively "fly by the seat of our pants" than to coast predictably through formal, dictum-oriented sessions. Therapy with this family also requires us to discard some of our comfortable and habitual therapeutic strategies and to develop some creative and novel approaches. But from the moment we acknowledge the guarded and self-protective family system and the long-ingrained rules against talking, feeling and trusting, it becomes apparent that conventional counseling will not be productive with this family.

The counselor who has an eclectic familiarity and expertise with varied theoretical models and bases will likely have a broader and more flexible range of therapeutic tactics at his/her fingertips. The following suggestions are not meant to be replacements for existing skills or styles; rather they are specifically designed to be superimposed on those skills and styles already in place to augment effectiveness and versatility.

Techniques That Don't Work

Just words.

Techniques That Do Work

Conditional Tense Therapy

Traditional talking, feeling therapy is at best ineffective and at worst counterproductive in the face of a family system locked behind the barricades of *don't talk, feel* or *trust*. When we ask these people to come into counseling to talk about their feelings and trust us, we are asking them to betray everything they have learned, everything they believe to be true, everything they have operated on for years. We are asking them to dissolve the very cement that has held the family together, and that they cannot and will not do. Their resistance is not obstinacy; those rules represent their basic survival.

Rather than confront the rules head on, which leads only to frustration and despair for them and for us, we need to devise ways to allow them to break the rules without attacking the rules directly. We need to give them permission to talk and feel and trust within the confines of their guarded and closed communication system. We as therapists need to learn to think and talk in the conditional.

This simply means we learn not to ask direct questions. Our interactions with this family are best framed in the conditional tense. Queries like "What happened next?" or "How did you feel about that?" will invariably be met with bland defensiveness. "Nothing" and "Fine" are typical responses. This is not evasion or distortion; it is reality as this family sees and feels it according to their rules. They aren't allowed to talk and they aren't allowed to feel. They know if they do, the whole fragile fabric of their existence will be rent asunder.

On the other hand, questions like "If you knew that your husband had a drinking problem, what would be telling you that?" or "If you could guess what happened next, what would that be?" allow them to share the secrets without breaking the *don't talk* rule. The same holds true for feelings. "If you had to guess what you felt inside when that happened, what would that be?" or "If you knew the last time Dad's drinking embarrassed you, when would that have been?" lets them touch their own emotions without breaking the *don't feel* rule.

The family doesn't have to trust in order to begin to process what has been happening and how they have been feeling. We are only asking them to speculate on what *might* have been happening or how they *might* have been feeling. Phrases like "if you knew" and "if you had to guess" need to become an integral and automatic part of the chemical dependency family therapist's vocabulary. They may be subtle and simple, but they are the quickest and most effective wedges into the rigid shell the disease has constructed around the family. They save time and energy and pain, and they pave the path toward recovery in ways that months of conventional probing and processing cannot accomplish.

Sublimation

Sometimes the rules are so highly developed and so tightly webbed that the family will resist even the most openly and casually granted permission to speak and share. In that case our techniques need to become more sophisticated in order to provide them more leeway and safety. If it is too threatening to guess what they might be feeling, we distance them from the risk by asking them to guess what *someone else* might feel in their particular circumstances.

One woman described her drunken husband's request that she move to the driver's seat after an auto accident so that he could avoid being charged with Driving While Intoxicated. When she was asked directly how she felt about his demand, her answer was a mild, "Okay". Even when she was asked to guess how she might have felt if she *could* feel, her answer was still offhand: "Well, I didn't think I should have to do that . . ." But when she was given permission to guess how someone else might feel, she shouted, "Enraged!"

The blocks may be even deeper around factual information. The *don't talk* rule becomes so imbedded that family members literally train themselves to forget what has happened. The family with a chemically dependent member learns to lie, to themselves and to others, and the line between falsehood and truth becomes blurred and indistinguishable. When upheaval and chaos are the norm, people truly have to forget their history in order to continue to exist and function as human beings. Sometimes no amount of prodding seems able to evoke the memory, even when they are struggling to do so.

Unblocking Memories

At that impasse it may become necessary to assess which portion of the memory system is blocking retrieval of the missing information. As humans, we store memories as sights, as sounds and as feelings, and we give appropriate non-verbal clues when we are searching our memory banks for lost data. Most people literally "look for" lost visual information with eyes that dart upwards into corners or thin air. They "listen for" auditory memories with eyes that shift from side to side or a head that cocks to catch an imaginary sound. They hunch over and "go inside" themselves to search for stored emotions. If we are sensitive to the clues they are providing, we can unblock the memories with verbal cues. Sight images like "What do you see?" or "Can you lift the veil?" or "Will you go behind the curtain?" will release visual secrets. Sound metaphors like "What do you hear?" or "Whose voice is telling you not to speak?" will facilitate auditory retrieval. And questions like "What is going on inside your body?" may allow hidden feelings to escape.

It is important for us to be aware of our own cognitive styles as therapists before we attempt to address information retrieval in someone else. Most of us operate predominantly on a visual or auditory or emotional level, and a counselor who thinks and speaks in visual terms will be hard-pressed to challenge auditory or emotional retrieval blocks in another. "Can you see what I'm saying?" will never be an effective communication tool.

In order to help this family break its own rules, it may be necessary for us as therapists to break with our own traditional therapeutic dogmas and improvise around our habitual counseling tactics. This is a family trapped by a cunning, baffling and powerful disease, and it takes strong and innovative therapy to free them from their captivity.

Modelling

These are people who don't trust words. Their stories are an endless procession of empty threats and broken promises, of feelings denied and discounted, of events repressed and concealed. To approach them with words alone is to lose them at the outset.

Even as we enter the family at that first educational level we become models for a radically new way of dealing with their family history. We define the chaos and anguish they have been experiencing as a disease rather than a shame, as a physical phenomenon rather than a behavioral or moral stigma. We model rational and nonjudgmental consideration of symptoms rather than guilty confession or betrayal.

We may need to start by defining and modelling normal behavior, for until this family begins to conceive that what has been happening for them may not be normal, they will certainly be unable to imagine what feelings might be appropriate for them. The family that has got used to moving a "sleeping" father around in his chair much like a piece of furniture in order to pursue their own activities needs to be told that this doesn't happen in every family. The family that has learned to have no expectations about vacations or planned family ventures or even the time of the family dinner hour needs to understand that this is not necessarily acceptable for other families.

Before we begin emotional modelling we may also need to establish what might be normal for them to feel in their circumstances. These are people who have adapted to unpredictability and inconsistency. They have learned to accept the bizarre as normal, so not only do they lack any clear conception of what normal behavior is, they also have little idea of what normal feelings are. It is often necessary for the therapist to begin with personal and self-disclosive emotional revelation: "If that happened to me I would feel angry."

Only after some data base for normal behavior and feelings has been developed can emotional modelling begin. At the feeling level modelling is tieing body to words. A good chemical dependency family therapist probably needs to be part actor. The theatrics do not detract from the therapy. They enhance it. We don't talk to them about a feeling; we show them. They have disconnected feeling words from what has been happening inside their bodies; they have denied what is going on emotionally for them. They have pretended that they couldn't feel at all for so long that they have, in fact, become numb and unfeeling. It's not enough to talk to them about their anger. The word anger may be totally meaningless for them. We must make their anger tangible and visible for them by demonstrating it ourselves, with clenched jaw, raised voice, tightened muscles and frowning face. We must teach them not only what they have been feeling or what they might have been feeling had they allowed those emotions to exist. We also need to teach them how to feel again. That process starts for them with our role modelling feelings for them, literally saying to them, "This is how I look and behave when I am feeling angry. This is how it is for normal people to feel and act."

Modelling allows families to begin to feel at a distance. It lets them see in another what they might be experiencing themselves under their pretense and control. Feelings must become safe and acceptable and able to be contemplated before they can be owned and expressed.

Sculpturing

Sculpturing is a logical extension of modelling. To sculpture is to paint a picture with bodies and objects. It makes feelings and dynamics long ignored and buried come alive. Sculpturing is dramatic, but it takes drama to penetrate the impoverished, frozen effect and the stilted, tangled structure that have become the family style. Again, these are people who don't trust words. Telling them what has been happening to them will be met with ambivalence and confusion; showing them will circumvent the verbal barriers and trigger insight and understanding.

The empty chair is the core of the sculpturing technique. It is the empty chair that shows the family visually the true composition of the family constellation. The empty chair literally hits them in the face with what has been missing and hidden up until now in the family equation. It provides the basis for a different and more accurate portrait of family interaction and a new focus for feelings. And it is the mental image of sneaking behind the empty chair, of creeping behind the back of the illness in order to save a life, that first gives the family permission and freedom to pursue the risk of intervention.

It is a natural progression from the counselor's solitary modelling of feelings to the family's sculpturing their own emotions. The therapist's modus operandi become "Don't tell me; show me." At first the family may seem reluctant and uncomfortable, but with guidance they will become familiar with expressing themselves in actions rather than in the words that have betrayed them so often in the past.

Sculpturing allows the family to make connections between behavior and feelings; it allows them to unfetter emotions that have long been imprisoned. When we attempt to tell them how much they have adjusted to the chemically dependent person and what an emotional toll that adjustment has taken on them, they tend to minimize their investment and dismiss their "walking on eggshells" around the chemically dependent person as inconsequential and unextraordinary. But when they are made to tiptoe around the empty chair for only a few moments they can feel for themselves their muscular strain; they can readily perceive the source of their tension and exhaustion, and they can begin to experience at a physical level the price they have paid as *adjusters.* When they are asked to guard the empty chair with outstretched arms to keep others, playing the parts of drinking and/or using friends or the drug itself, from darting in to reach the chair, they can identify clearly the frustration and helplessness that result from their controlling, protecting efforts as *enablers.* And when the drug and friends breech the feeble barricade their solitary efforts have raised, they can understand the guilt and inadequacy and failure that fall to them as the disease's *victims.*

Sculpturing allows feelings to be experienced in their true intensity. Anger verbalized by this family is anger glossed over and discounted. But anger expressed by standing and shaking a fist at the empty chair is anger witnessed and validated. Embarrassment is offered in apologetic and half-obscured words; a person crouched beside the empty chair demonstrates dramatically the gnawing denigration of shame. The trapped, enmeshed tangle of emotion is clearly visible when one person's arms are locked and struggling under the arms of that empty chair.

Finally, sculpturing not only identifies and releases repressed feelings; sculpturing also initiates the affective and structural changes that precipitate family recovery. When the family member kneeling or crouching in front of the empty chair in a posture of helplessness and hopelessness moves to stand over the chair, the family's powerlessness becomes power in a physical sense. And when the family forms a ring around the empty chair and weighs their numbers against the chair's isolation, their power over the disease is visually affirmed and augmented.

Sculpturing allows the family to recognize and acknowledge and ventilate at a concrete level; it moves emotion from the realm of the theoretical and concep-tual to the realm of the personal and possible. The family establishes coherent and congruent ties between what they have been doing and what they have been feeling, and they carve for themselves a model for change.

Humor

For the family with a chemically dependent member, life is deadly serious business, and quite probably nothing has seemed funny or amusing to them for years. Humor will be met at the very least by resistance or revulsion; more likely humor will not even register with this family. Their ability to experience happy feelings has been frozen and repressed along with their pain and hurt, and their reaction to humor is typically deadpan. Although some of what has happened to the family, and some of the things they themselves have done, are indeed funny, to laugh about those things is to insult them. When people in Al-Anon chuckle about being "sicker than he is", the family still in the throes of their own suffering feels belittled and threatened.

Yet every therapist knows that in laughter lie the seeds of wellness. Most laughter at self is retrospective; it derives from relief that this never has to happen again. The family's ability to laugh with and at themselves is a valid measure of the progress they have made toward recovery. In fact, laughter can play a pivotal role in initiating family recovery.

We must simply do with humor what we do with everything else for this family — we must define it for them. It is often enough to warn them, "Now I'm going to tease you for a moment," or "Now I'm going to tell you something that may make you laugh . . ."

Once again, the family needs permission to feel and respond. Once again, we need to be sensitive to who these people are and where they are coming from in order to use our therapeutic tools effectively.

Afterword

To be an intervention counselor takes a special kind of love and a special brand of courage. Intervention counseling is often painful, sometimes sad, frequently exhausting, rarely predictable, never easy. Interventions may be peak counseling experiences, but the road to intervention for the counselor is often paved with hard-won self-knowledge and unexpected self-revelation, and caring, giving and sharing beyond the ordinary. It requires of us dedication and tenacity and detachment all at once. It asks us to give the best of ourselves in the face of self-doubt and fear.

But the rewards can be overwhelming, too. To be an instrument for saving a life, to help a family move from guilt and anger and pain toward peace and hope — these are gifts life offers to very few. They are both wonderful privileges and awesome responsibilities.

I hope this book leaves you with enhanced skills and heightened potential to change families and save lives. May you use them wisely and well, and may you be blessed along your way.

Suggested Resources

Alcoholism: A Treatable Disease. Pamphlet. Minneapolis, Minnesota: Johnson Institute, 1972.
A brief overview of the symptoms and progression of the disease of alcoholism, including treatment options and recovery.

Cocaine. Film. St. Louis, Missouri: Post Productions, 1983.
A comprehensible explanation of the physical and psychological consequences of cocaine use and abuse.

The Disease Concept of Alcoholism. Film. St. Louis, Missouri: Gary Whiteaker Company, 1981.
A practical synopsis of alcoholism research that outlines the course of the disease of alcoholism and presents evidence of metabolic differences in the alcoholic body supporting the existence of a true disease. Must viewing for everyone contemplating intervention.

Drews, Toby Rice, **Getting Them Sober,** Volume I. South Plainfield, New Jersey: Bridge Publishing Company, 1980.

A helpful collection of concrete suggestions and strategies to guide family members away from enabling and toward detachme. t.

Drug Dependency. Film. Glendal , California: Aims Media.

A clear description of the symptoms and progression of dependency on drugs other than alcohol.

The Enablers. Film. Minneapolis, Minnesota: Johnson Institute.

A dramatization of the progression of alcoholism, which portrays the destructive results of enabling on all members of the family, including the chemically dependent person.

Gold, Mark S., M.D., **800-COCAINE.** New York: Bantam Books, 1984.

A discussion of the use and abuse of cocaine, including physical and psychological effects of the drug and options for treatment and recovery.

I'll Quit Tomorrow, Parts I, II and III. Film. Minneapolis, Minnesota: Johnson Institute.

An older film which shows both an unsuccessful and a successful intervention.

Intervention. Film. Minneapolis, Minnesota: Johnson Institute.

A reenactment of an intervention involving the family in **The Enablers** and designed to follow that film. Provides insight into the process of intervention and models possible roles in actual intervention for various members of the intervention team at several different relationship levels to the chemically dependent person.

Johnson, Vernon E., **I'll Quit Tomorrow.** San Francisco, California: Harper and Row, 1980.

A classic manual dealing with alcoholism and treatment at physical, mental and spiritual levels. Includes a chapter on the Johnson model of intervention.

Kellerman, Joseph L. **Alcoholism: A Merry-Go-Round Called Denial.** Pamphlet. Center City, Minnesota: Hazelden, 1980.

A brief discussion of the pivotal role denial plays in the disease process.

Kellerman, Joseph L., **A Guide for the Family of an Alcoholic.** Pamphlet. Center City, Minnesota: Hazelden, 1980.

A short summary of family patterns useful for defining enabling and supporting detachment.

Mann, Peggy, **Pot Safari: A Visit to the Top Marijuana Researchers in the U.S.** New York: Woodmere Press, 1982.

A detailed survey of the physical and pharmacological dynamics of marijuana use and abuse.

Meagher, M. David, **Beginning of A Miracle: How to Intervene with the Alcoholic or Addicted Person.** Pompano Beach, Florida: Health Communications, 1987.

A detailed look at addiction with the intervention process as the first step to recovery.

Milam, James R. and Katherine Ketchum. **Under the Influence.** Seattle, Washington: Madrona Publishers, 1981.

A comprehensive description of the disease of alcoholism, emphasizing the effects on the body and brain and the criteria for diagnosis of the illness.

Pot. Film. St. Louis, Missouri: Gary Whiteaker Company.

An informative presentation of the physical and psychological effects of marijuana use and abuse.

Sedativism. Film. St. Louis, Missouri: Gary Whiteaker Company, 1981.

An understandable definition of cross-addiction and the role of all mood-altering chemicals in the disease of chemical dependency.

Sherman, Paul, **Intervention in the Workplace.** Pompano Beach, Florida: Health Communicatons, 1987.

An in-depth study of chemical dependency in the executive office and how the organization can intervene.

This is Al-Anon. Pamphlet. New York: Al-Anon Family Group Headquarters, 1981 revised.

An introduction to Al-Anon as a self-help support group for affected family members.

Wegscheider, Sharon. **Another Chance: Hope and Health for Alcoholic Families.** Palo Alto, California: Science and Behavior Books, Inc., 1980.

An in-depth exploration of the alcoholic family system, including roles, rules, patterns and suggestions for recovery. Contains a discussion of intervention.

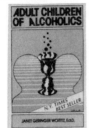